A COLLECTION OF RANDOM RHYMES

MALLIKA SEN

Made with ♥ on the Notion Press Platform
www.notionpress.com

To Amma and Baba.

For being my constant light at the end of every dark tunnel.

Contents

Contents

1. A Collection of Random Rhymes

A notebook filled with scribbled lines.

Snippets of thoughts and tales untold.

Forgotten somewhere, in a closet closed.

Embraced by cobwebs, in dust behold,

this small collection of random rhymes.

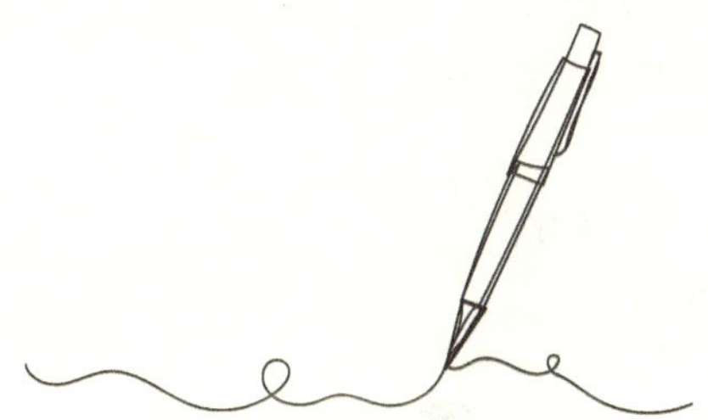

2. Remember When

Remember when,
accustomed faces fade a little
and memories grow old.
Remember when,
echoes of laughter
linger late into the night.
Remember when,
shared jokes and wine,
bring a smile; a thought to mind.
Remember then,
talks about everything.
Saying nothing, star gazing.
Remember.
Somewhere, someday,
the time we spent.

3. Home

Home is a feeling.
It has no walls.
Not where I was born,
nor where I sleep.
It's the people I love
and places I remember.
It's in puppy snuggles,
warm hugs, and giggles.
The feeling of peace.
A space to breathe deep.
It's in the warmth of the sunshine
and in lazy summer nights.
It's in the wind, and in the rain,
and in cups of hot tea
after long, weary days.
Home is a feeling
I carry with me.

4. A Wanderer's Tale

There was a man, a wanderer.

He sat down beside me, by the river yonder.

And looked at me with wise, old eyes;

and smiled a smile that made me cry.

The lives we lead are but a lie, said he.

For we live in search of blissful eternity.

And such a thing no man can see.

Love is a fragile creature,

on gossamer wings she flies.

Touch her and break the spell.

For all that lives, one day will die.

5. A Little Corner of My Mind

There's a place I go to everyday.
A quiet, peaceful space
in some little corner of my mind.
Here I can wash away the day,
the weariness and disarray.
And file my waking hours away,
in neat folders, labelled in grey.
The good and bad,
the happy and the sad.
To be taken out someday,
stories from my yesterdays.
Dusted off and read again.

6. Masquerade

A face of stone she wears outside.
A mask behind, where shadows lie.
Shattered glass, like broken dreams.
Watch where you step, listen as she screams.
She builds walls around; a fortress of ice.
Let no one reach the pain inside.

❡

A crack in the plaster, a chink in the wall.
A peephole, a window into her soul.
So lost and alone, so far from home.
A figure in the darkness, a flicker of light.
Can you see it when she cries?
The child who hides within her eyes.

7. Karuna

If there is one feeling
I want to hold on to,
it is kindness.
I don't want to lose that
in the pursuit of intellect.
For what are we
without a little softness?
A little compassion?
We can learn everything
the world knows,
and then some.
But if we harden our souls
we will be none the wiser.

8. 3 A.M. Thoughts

Musings of a weary mind;
wanderings of a different kind.
Pondering the here and now;
wondering what I missed somehow.
Waiting for the day to break;
watching as the shadows play.
Lying here with unshed tears;
trying to suppress the fears.
Hoping when the darkness fades,
morning brings a brighter day.

9. Soft Lies and Laughter

I would like to believe

in a world of dreams.

No sadness, no tears,

no pain, and no fears.

We've had enough of those.

Let's take away reality,

send life on a different journey.

Where everything is magical,

made to order, perfect.

Of beauty so great,

of silence so complete.

Of fairies' lairs and dancing bears,

talking trees and whispering bees.

Of tinkling laughter on faraway shores.

Play a game of catch with the clouds.

Reach for the stars, sprinkle them around.

Where every story has a happy ending,

and there are no broken hearts that need mending.

Here dreams are reality,

and wishes come true.

When we wake up,

the memories will do.

A merry tune,

a joyous tale,

and silent echoes of

soft lies and laughter.

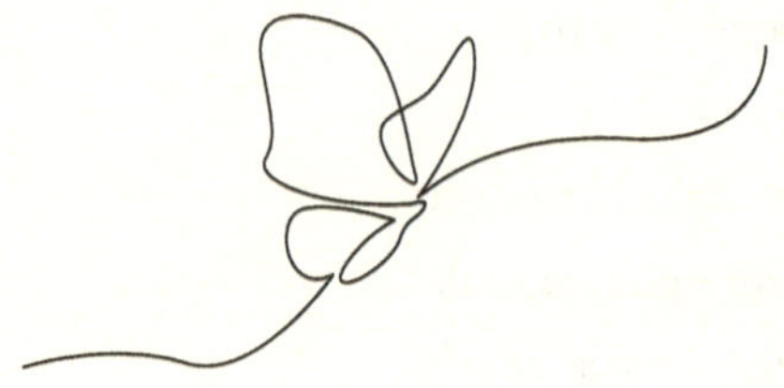

10. Pandemonium

What do you do

when your thoughts become so loud

that they drown out every other noise?

When memories clamour behind your eyes.

When everything inside you

is running the four minute mile.

Where do you go to find silence?

When there is nothing but screaming inside your mind.

11. Maya

The impermanence of life
fills me with a sense of wonder.
That we are beings defined by transience,
and yet, in our fleeting time in this form,
we strive for stability,
resist change,
aim for immortality.

12. Narasimha

Walking with two faces.
One turned towards the light,
the other living in shadows.
Forever opposed,
conflict must follow.
Torn in two.
Flesh, skin, and bone.
A part of me and a part of you.
Forges a new being.
An entity of the twilight zone.

13. We Could Be Better

We choose rage over reason,
hatred over compassion.
Rhetoric over fact,
conspiracy over science.

❡

Turning a blind eye,
looking the other way.
From acts of violence
in word or deed
at our every doorstep.

❡

We don't stand up for what is right;
fearing backlash from all that is wrong.
Celebrating the differences,
instead of common goals.
We mock diversity.

❡

Cocooned in the comfort of the familiar.
It is "them" versus "us"!
Failing to see what's in plain sight.
That there is no "them", only "us".

14. Star Crossed

For years I searched
for a glimpse of you
in every face I met.
When chance decided
that we should cross paths,
all I could see was the crowd.

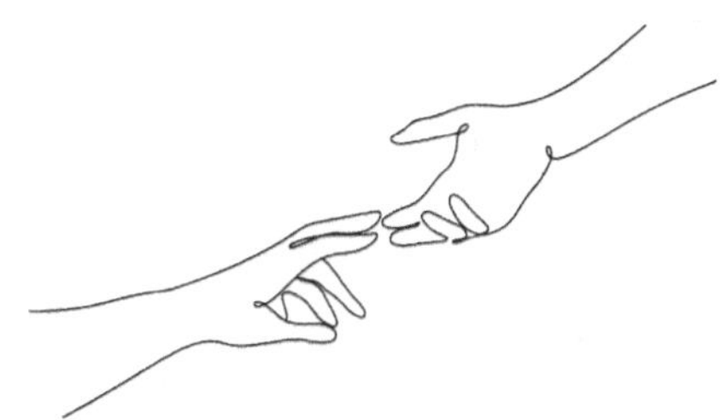

15. Changes

A wise person once said,
"Nothing is permanent but change".
How I hate those words!
Everytime I have to move on,
I leave a part of me behind.
Torn from my soul,
another little hole.
But then onwards time does roll.
The rough, cutting edges
are smoothed away.
To make place for new days,
new ways, and new beginnings.

16. The Kind of Me I Wish to Be

I will be free!

Have no one telling me how to be.

How to speak, or how to move.

When to laugh and when to cry.

When to love, or when to leave.

I will be free.

There's no other way I'm willing to be.

Won't be one on a list;

can't follow the crowd.

No waiting to be heard,

or stopping to be seen.

I will be me.

Love me or hate me,

but just let me be.

Nothing to define me,

confine me.

Don't try to stop me.

Don't fit a frame around me.

Neither truth, nor lies.

No prayers or curses.

Sinner or saint.

My choice.

My life.

This is me.

17. The Aisle of Forgotten Souls

What is wrong and what is right?
Is it all so black and white?
Or are there many shades of grey
as you try to find your way?
Thoughts that tangle up inside,
give you room and space to hide.
In a world of false morality,
falling from high grounds a fatality.
Rules that you must obey
if society's code should have its say.
No room for the black sheep.
Discarded, disregarded, hear them weep.
Come with me; let's take a walk
along the aisle of forgotten souls.

18. Where Love Lives

Where does love go to die?
After the pain and anger subside.
When you've run out of tears
and the chapter is closed.

¶

Where does love go to hide?
Under the blankets, buried away.
In crumpled papers
and torn bits of love letters.

¶

Where does love go to rest?
In the quiet spaces of your mind.
In the steady, beating rhythm
of your healing heart.

19. 52 Blue

(The Loneliest Whale)

Imagine the vastness of the oceans.
The blue that surrounds you.
Imagine calling into that void.
Calling, and calling, and calling.
For an eternity with no response.
No answering cry.
Not a whisper.
Nothing.
Would you call into a cave?
Just to hear your own echo?
Pretend that someone out there hears you?
Sees you?
What would it be like
to live a life with a different voice?
One that calls into the void,
and calls, and calls, and calls.
An endless search with no reward.
Would you stop calling?
Would your voice slowly fade away?
Into the vast blue.

Into nothingness.

20. A Love Letter to Life

My life has been simple,
far easier than most.
I've wanted for nothing
that this world can hold.
A roof overhead,
warm blankets in bed.
A pleasant smile
and curious eyes.
Laughter and tears,
great love and fears.
The pain of loss,
or an abundance of joy.
Life has given to me
all these and more.
My heart is full,
as is my cup.
So I'll raise a toast,
"To all that there is,
and all that will be".

21. Photographs

I have photographs from everywhere I go;
keepsakes of places I used to know.
Cosy cafes and wide open fields,
sunset viewpoints and old cobbled streets.

❡

Photographs from days gone by;
snapshots of a different time.
Ma and Pa when they were young.
The world they knew, the life they lived.

❡

Photographs of childhood friends,
the kind that always make you smile.
Were we really quite so small?
With big toothless grins,
dirty clothes, and bruised shins.

❡

Photographs of you and me
captured moments of happiness.
This one where we laughed until we cried,
or this one that caught us by surprise.

❡

I have photographs from everywhere I go.
Reminding me that time must flow.

These photographs will stay with me.

Forever precious memories.

22. My Ikigai

I was asked this question
a while ago.
What lessons I'd learned;
what values I hold?
It took me but a moment
of reflection, and I said,
there is this one thing
my parents told me,
"Be kind".
And so, I try to be.

23. When All Things Are Said and Done

There are so many things I've wanted to say,

so many ideas cluttered away.

Waiting for my words to speak

them into sweet release.

But then a wayward thought did stray.

Hadn't it all been said and done

by so many who have come before?

Wiser minds than mine for sure.

How could my words even begin to compare

with all the thinkers in the world today?

And so I was quiet, my voice unheard.

Until one day a timid spark arose.

Perhaps there would be someone near?

Who had thoughts like my own,

they never dared share?

And if only I'd gather the courage to speak,

they'd be happy to listen and talk with me.

And finally our words would be free.

24. Small Talk

Just a chit chat
on a rainy day.
Nothing much prepared.
Musings on this and that,
over cups of steaming chai.
Ma and I.
Sitting cross legged,
cushions on our laps.
Watching the raindrops
pitter-patter, pitter-patter.
A little bird fluffs itself
on the windowsill.
Ma laughs, pointing at it.
Shushing me,
lest it should become aware,
of the two pairs of curious eyes
watching its little charade.

25. The Golden Hour

It's one of my favourite memories
of Baba and me.
Surrounded by the sea
in the golden hour.
Wading into shimmering waters.
Warm sunlight on our faces,
the wind in our hair.
Bobbing gently on the waves;
seaweed brushing against our feet.
And when I turned towards him,
he had the most brilliant smile I'd ever seen.
My heart! What I would have given
to hold on to that moment.
So I took a deep breath
and soaked it all in.
The sun, the waves,
the endless sea.
Holding hands,
Baba and me.

26. Puppy Love

Puppy love.
The best kind there is!
Mornings filled with stolen kisses.
Warm breath on my face.
Wet nosed,
slobbery love.

¶

A thump, thump, thump,
like the beat of my heart.
Excited snuffles.
Waggity love.
A puppy's love!
The best kind there is!

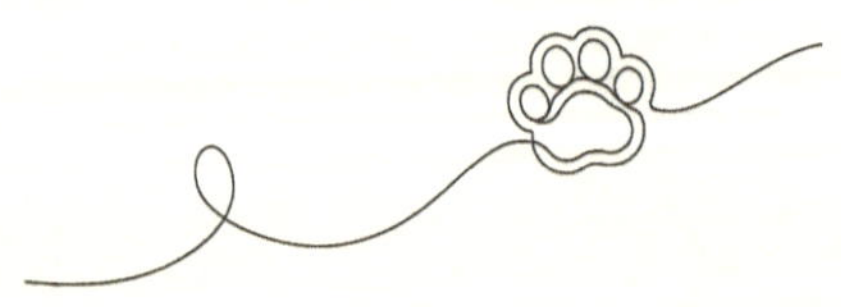

27. Swallow Song

I nearly trod on it,
buried in the wet.
This tiny, feathered thing,
beaten down by the storm.

❡

Held within cupped palms.
Covered in mud,
barely alive.
It did not stir.

❡

Swathed in warm towels;
placed in a small box.
The rise and fall of every breath,
some faint sign of life.

❡

Waiting out the storm,
this wee swallow and I.
Two bedraggled souls
hoping for their miracle.

❡

The day crept in
and all around was quiet.
I heard a little chirp;

my heart sang with delight.

❡

Sat on my shoulder,

snoozing in my hair.

It did not wish to leave,

so there I stayed awhile.

❡

Hopped on to my hand,

fluffed and preened.

Spread its wings out wide,

and flew into a bright blue sky.

28. The Last

A kiss, a dance,

a sweet refrain.

A laugh, a toast,

and a wave goodbye.

A train, a stop,

amidst drops of rain.

A stand, a line,

a warrior's clarion call.

A cry, a prayer,

and a hope against hope.

A word, a breath,

a beating heart.

A tale, a time,

a fading memory.

A chance, a try,

and a dark night sky.

The one standing,

smiled and walked away.

An Encore

On Poetry

Some poems soothe your mind;

while some get you thinking.

Others speak of tales of woe;

another tells of happy times.

Most of them are written in rhyme.

There's a few that even break this rule.

Poets, we're a motley crew.

Read by many, understood by few.